WHAT THE FUTURE HOLDS

THE FUTURE OF ENTERTAINMENT:

FROM MOVIES TO VIRTUAL REALITY

BY M. M. EBOCH
CONTENT CONSULTANT:
PETER C. BISHOP, PH.D., APF
TEACHTHEFUTURE.ORG
HOUSTONFUTURES.ORG

CAPSTONE PRESS
a capstone imprint

Capstone Captivate is published by Capstone Press, an imprint of Capstone.
1710 Roe Crest Drive, North Mankato, Minnesota 56003
www.capstonepub.com

Copyright © 2020 by Capstone. All rights reserved. No part of this publication may be reproduced in whole or in part, or stored in a retrieval system, or transmitted in any form or by any means, electronic, mechanical, photocopying, recording, or otherwise, without written permission of the publisher.

Library of Congress Cataloging-in-Publication Data
Names: Eboch, M. M., author.
Title: The future of entertainment : from movies to virtual reality / by M.M. Eboch ; Content Consultant ; Peter C. Bishop, Ph.D., APF. Description: North Mankato : Capstone Press, 2020. | Series: What the future holds | Includes bibliographical references and index. | Audience: Ages 8-11 | Audience: Grades 4-6 | Summary: "From stage productions to television to movies, humans have always been entertained by a good story. But how might entertainment change in the future? From immersive virtual reality games to social media with 3-D holograms, readers can find out what cool new technologies might change the way they are entertained"— Provided by publisher.
Identifiers: LCCN 2019043966 (print) | LCCN 2019043967 (ebook) | ISBN 9781543592214 (hardcover) | ISBN 9781496666253 (paperback) | ISBN 9781543592252 (pdf)
Subjects: LCSH: Amusements—Technological innovations—Juvenile literature. | Virtual reality—Juvenile literature. | Motion pictures—Juvenile literature.
Classification: LCC GV1203 .E26 2020 (print) | LCC GV1203 (ebook) | DDC 790.1/922—dc23
LC record available at https://lccn.loc.gov/2019043966
LC ebook record available at https://lccn.loc.gov/2019043967

Image Credits
Alamy: Andrew Barker, 23, (bottom), ClassicStock, 5, Dino Fracchia, 31, John D. Ivanko, 33, The Hollywood Archive/PictureLux, 13; iStockphoto: sturti, 11; Newscom: Avalon.red/PacificCoastNews/Joe Sutter, 39, Kyodo, 19, YNA/Yonhap News, 9, (top), ZUMA Press/Ash Knotek, 37, ZUMA Press/Jeff Gritchen, 23, (top), ZUMA Press/Martha Asencio Rhine, 35; Shutterstock: Andrey_Popov, 25, BOULENGER Xavier, 43, Douglas Olivares, 21, khoamartin, Cover, LesPalenik, 9, (bottom), misszin, 15, OHishiapply, 29, Prostock-studio, 27, Richman Photo, 41, Stuart Jenner, 7; U.S. Air Force photo by John Ingle, 17

Design Elements
Shutterstock: nanmulti, Zeynur Babayev

TABLE OF CONTENTS

INTRODUCTION
THE CHANGING FACE OF ENTERTAINMENT 4

CHAPTER 1
WHAT IS JUST AHEAD? 8

CHAPTER 2
WHAT DOES THE FUTURE HOLD? 20

CHAPTER 3
WHAT IS WAY OUT THERE? 32

TIMELINE 44
GLOSSARY 46
READ MORE 47
INTERNET SITES 47
INDEX 48

Words in bold are in the glossary.

INTRODUCTION

THE CHANGING FACE OF ENTERTAINMENT

How did people entertain themselves 100 years ago? They read books or played board games. People played instruments or listened to music on record players. Hollywood was making the first full-length movies, which were black and white and silent. You could only watch them in a theater.

Movies with sound started in 1927. By the late 1920s to the early 1930s, people gathered around radios to hear actors perform stories. The first televisions went on sale in 1939. Full-color movies were common by the 1940s. Over time, TV and movie images got sharper. Color became more realistic.

Many people got their first home computers in the 1980s. Computers brought new types of games. The first computer games were simple. Players batted a ball or tried to shoot at a very simple spaceship.

In the 1930s and 1940s, family entertainment included books, games, and listening to the radio.

FACT
The first computer game was created for the 1940 World's Fair. People competed with the computer to pick up sticks. The computer won 90 percent of the games.

Over time, computers got better, smaller, and less expensive. Now they are in our phones and watches. Computer games are more complex. The internet brings us videos and games in seconds.

What might the future of entertainment hold? Futurists attempt to answer that question. **Futures studies** is the study of possible and probable future **scenarios**. This is not simply guessing. Experts in the field consider many factors. They look at history to learn from the past. They consider current beliefs people have. They ask what people want to happen. They look at what is possible now and what may be possible soon.

In entertainment, a few things have stayed the same—people like stories, music, and games. The future probably won't change that. Today we enjoy stories in the form of books, movies, TV shows, and plays. We listen to music live or on electronic devices. We can play board games, video games, and sports. In the future, there will likely be even more ways we can make and enjoy stories and games.

Who would have predicted 100 years ago that people would one day read books on computerized e-readers?

FACT
In 1948, Americans could watch TV shows from four companies on four channels. Today there are far more than 1,000 channels.

CHAPTER 1
WHAT IS JUST AHEAD?

Television is one form of entertainment that has changed a lot. Early TVs were small boxes that showed images in black and white. The first color TV sets were sold in 1954. They had 15-inch (38-centimeter) screens and cost more than $1,000.

Since then, screens keep getting bigger, and their images get sharper. One new TV from Samsung is 12 feet (3.6 meters) wide. It can be made in any shape or size.

Sound has gotten better too. **Three-dimensional** (3-D) sound systems bring sound similar to that of movie theaters to your home. The speakers are aimed at different parts of the room. They can imitate a plane flying overhead. Most people don't yet have giant screens with 3-D sound systems. But every few years, screens get a little bigger, and sound gets better.

TV designs have changed a lot, from clunky box sets to Samsung's new customizable flat screen, "The Wall."

TUBES TO CRYSTALS

Early TVs were more than 1 foot (30 cm) thick. They were filled with tubes, wires, and speakers. These things turned the TV signal into sound and pictures. The 1990s brought flat-screen TVs that were less than 4 inches (10-cm) thick. They used liquid crystals instead of tubes.

PART OF THE SHOW

People used to simply watch TV. A show came on at a certain time each week. You had to be there, or you'd miss it. Then recording devices let us save shows for later. Now streaming channels, such as Netflix and Hulu, give thousands of options at any moment. We can watch an entire season of a show in one day. We never have to skip an episode.

Some shows even let us change the story. These interactive shows let you decide what happens next. Netflix introduced the first of these in 2017. *Puss in Boots* and *Buddy Thunderstruck* offered simple choices. Now these stories are getting more complex. The future will show how far they can go.

Allowing viewers to make choices as to how the story line goes makes TV more like a video game. Will engaging viewers keep people watching? Or will viewers miss being able to talk to one another about a show if they're all watching different versions of a show?

Choosing story lines lets people watching the same show see different plotlines unfold.

People like to discuss movies and TV shows. Social media makes this easy. Social media sites such as Facebook, Twitter, Instagram, and Pinterest are very popular. Now 86 percent of Americans use social media every day. Fans get to discuss shows in new ways. They can tweet their feelings as they watch. They can share fun clips. Fans can find other people who love their favorite shows. They can join discussion groups.

Fans can even tell the writers what they want to happen. Shows sometimes change based on fan feedback. That can be good or bad. For example, the musical TV show *Glee* started writing episodes to please fans. But those twists didn't always fit the overall story. In the end, the show lost many fans.

Today people want their ideas to be heard. Companies that make TV shows are listening. How will fan feedback change the future of entertainment?

The cast of the TV show *Glee*

FACT

Facebook had 1 million users in its first year. In 2010, it had more than 500 million users. That number reached 2 billion in 2018.

13

BRINGING THE ACTION TO LIFE

Some people don't simply want to watch a story or even choose what happens next. They want to be part of the story. **Virtual reality** (VR) uses computers to create a world that feels real. A headset provides the sights and sounds. The cheapest option, Google Cardboard, can cost less than $15. It works with a smartphone to provide 3-D visuals.

Other options are fancier. They make it seem more like you're part of the action. Along with a headset, they have special gloves that makes it feel as though you are touching and moving real objects. A vest makes it feel like you are moving up and down. Get near a virtual lava pit and the vest can make you feel a blast of hot air.

Right now, VR that appeals to several senses is expensive. You might find it in a gaming center. The next 10 years may bring this kind of fuller VR experience into the home.

The Google Cardboard VR goggles work by inserting a smartphone into the front of the device.

FACT
You can see objects from some museums through VR goggles at home. The British Museum in London and the American Museum of Natural History in New York City have shared their collections in VR.

One important part of VR is **haptic feedback**. This adds the sense of touch to your experience. Haptic feedback can give many sensations. You can feel shapes and texture. You might feel pressure, pain, hot, and cold.

A small mobile device can have haptic feedback. When a phone vibrates, that's haptic feedback. VR haptic feedback can be much more advanced. It can send pulses through the screen to your fingertips. You can feel texture, such as water ripples or pebbles.

A bodysuit with VR and haptic feedback lets a person feel things all over the body. The military uses these suits for training now. Someday they might be commonly used for fun. The haptics industry is expected to be worth more than $19 billion by 2025. Haptic VR devices may become as common as smartphones.

FACT
Some VR apps help people face their fears, such as the fear of heights, in virtual reality.

U.S. Airforce cadets train to fly the T-38C Talon jet using VR technology.

Like VR, **augmented reality** (AR) creates a new world. It too uses computer-generated objects. But AR objects are layered on top of the real world. Digital maps set games in your neighborhood. The *Pokémon Go* game is a good example of AR. It lets players catch imaginary monsters around their own towns. A Harry Potter game turns the player's town into Hogwarts. Now AR games are played with phones or tablets. One day AR devices could even be implanted into contact lenses. Then we would be fully immersed in an AR world.

Some people say VR and AR separate us from our real lives. That can be a welcome escape if you're, say, stuck in a dentist's chair. But it could also isolate people from others.

Maybe it will just change the way humans connect. We'll find out as more people use VR and AR in the coming years. As with most things, it likely depends on how the technology is used.

A *Pokémon Go* player spots a character to capture in Osaka, Japan.

FACT

One concern with AR is that people may be able to **hack** AR games. Then they could see your room, record you talking, or even make you walk into a wall.

CHAPTER 2

WHAT DOES THE FUTURE HOLD?

Technology tends to get better, less expensive, and more common over time. For example, the Apple App Store opened in 2008 with 500 apps. By 2017, the store had 2.1 million apps. This type of growth could happen with AR and VR too. In 10 to 20 years, you may be able to hang out with digital ghosts or visit a virtual dinosaur park from the comfort of your living room.

You can also learn with VR. Many experts think kids learn better if they're playing. One program takes students on VR field trips to the Amazon rain forest. They float down the Amazon River and over a waterfall. Students can take pictures of wildlife in the game as they learn about the animals. As the systems get cheaper, more schools could use them. Kids might study ancient Rome by touring an old Roman city and interacting with people and places there. They could even explore the surface of the moon.

Imagine taking a boat down the Amazon River from the safety and comfort of your computer screen.

FACT
The first smartphones came out in 2007 and 2008. Now more than 2.5 billion people in the world have smartphones.

SHAKE UP THE THEATER

There is a huge trend right now to create virtual experiences that feel more like real life. But this trend isn't new. 3-D movies have made watching movies more exciting for viewers for almost 100 years. These types of movies are getting more and more realistic. Today people can feel as though they're right in the middle of the action. Some theaters even give viewers VR headsets.

Someday movies at theaters may use haptics as well. Movies could become more like amusement park rides. In a motion simulator ride, the seats move. You may only actually move a few inches, but you feel as though you're flying through space. The seats can imitate falling or shaking in an earthquake. Smells, mist, or fog may spray over the riders.

It costs a lot to add these features. The people who make movies would have to design them with haptic feedback. In the next 10 to 20 years, some theaters might try adding more VR and haptic feedback. If they do, more theaters could follow. VR and haptic feedback could become common for home TVs as well.

Riders on the Disney VR ride Soarin' Around the World can experience what feels like a flight around the world, including soaring through the mists of Niagara Falls.

SMART MACHINES

There are billions of devices connected to the internet now, from toys to self-driving cars. They use the **Global Positioning System** (GPS) to see where you go and how fast you're moving. Some can be worn, such as smart watches. Sensors in these devices may check your pulse or get other feedback from your body. A smart watch can tell if you are going for a jog. It records how fast you run and the music you like. The more you use a device, the more it learns about how you behave and what you like. This type of technology can be made part of entertainment devices too.

Computers and devices that learn and respond have artificial intelligence (AI). Your devices can already learn where you go, what you do, and what you like. In the future, sensors in your clothes and devices may track your emotions. Your device could provide the right music or movie for your mood or time of day.

Today's smart watches can track heart rate, speed, calories burned, and even map out your exercise route. It can be synced up to other devices as well.

FACT
Today most devices offer suggestions with spoken or written words. Someday more might make suggestions through **holograms**.

Computers are even being trained to understand emotion. Game designers could one day be able to track every moment of game play to see what works best for a gamer. What do players like? What annoys them? If a game senses you are confused or frustrated, it could offer help. If you're getting bored, the game might offer an exciting twist. If you are too anxious, the game could give you a break.

Scientists are exploring other ways to use this technology. The Massachusetts Institute of Technology in Cambridge, Massachusetts, has several projects that study people over time. Devices record what makes people happy or unhappy. This information shows how we can improve our surroundings or our behavior. A company could change its office design to make workers happier. Doctors could decorate their offices so patients have less stress. This tech could be used in concert halls, theaters, and sports arenas too. Devices could even nudge people to go outside, since that makes most people happy.

Computers could one day understand the emotions behind almost every human expression.

FACT
Advertisers also want to study people's emotions. Then they can offer you what you are most likely to buy.

27

SMARTER GAMES

With AI and **machine learning**, games will be able to adapt as you play them. Characters in a game could change as you interact with them. The steps would change every time you play. Gamers would no longer be able to memorize steps to reach the next level.

Unfortunately, a smart game doesn't always make for more fun. Most games now involve storytelling. They are designed to give the player a specific experience. AI adds an element of chance. If the AI goes in strange directions, the story could fall apart. For now, game designers need to control that. They want games to feel real, but not have the endless options of reality.

Still, as AI advances in other areas, it may lead to new forms of gaming that humans have yet to imagine. AI could be able to change games so they never grow old. As AI improves and becomes more autonomous, it may start designing games itself.

Today gamers face off at competitions such as the Intel Game Time event in Bangkok, Thailand.

AI AND US

Some games even let players become the AI. You could play the role of a robot with artificial intelligence. You could develop your robot character in different ways. It could become an artist or fall in love. But the robot character would be controlled by someone playing a human character in the game. That gamer could wipe out the memories of your character. Then you would have to start over again.

These games raise questions about power and freedom. They explore what it means to be a robot and what it means to be human. These could be important questions in the future. A 2016 survey showed that 24 percent of teens believed a robot would one day become their best friend. This could be true in the next 30 years. How might having robot friends affect real human interaction? Games that let people play as AI help us explore these issues.

DANGEROUS CONNECTIONS

Connecting devices to the internet has risks. Companies can learn all about you. They use this information to try to sell you things you don't really need. Some smart devices have flaws that can be hacked. Strangers may be able to see through your webcam or hear you talk. They could access private messages and **data** on your device.

Pal Robotics' robot, Reem, moves independently through a crowd in Milan, Italy, in 2017.

CHAPTER 3
WHAT IS WAY OUT THERE?

The farther into the future we look, the more difficult it is to predict what will happen. What might the world look like in 50 to 100 years? Might humans really have robot best friends?

You can already get a robot helper. A Chinese company, UBTECH, is about to release a robot called Walker. It is almost 5 feet (1.5 m) tall and shaped like a person. It can pick up objects and open doors. Other robots look more like computers that can move. Right now, these robots cost thousands of dollars. They could be used to help the elderly and people with disabilities. In the future, robots may also provide entertainment.

If robots become affordable enough, we could all have them. With AI, some robots are already learning to be more like people. They seem to have emotions. In some ways, they could feel like friends. But what if your robot stops working? You'd lose that connection, and it might make you sad.

UBTECH's robot, Walker, shows what it can do at a Las Vegas trade show.

33

KEEPING MEMORIES ALIVE

Technology can't stop death. But it can keep memories alive in new ways.

Computer-generated imagery (CGI) has been used in recent movies after actors have died. Past videos of the actors show their faces. A new actor speaks wearing **motion capture** technology. CGI combines the two. It looks like the dead actor is speaking the new lines. The Star Wars movie *Rogue One* used this so that two characters could appear when the actors playing them had either died or aged.

Companies have also used this tech to send dead singers on tour. A live band plays along with the artist's singing hologram. Holograms of singers Amy Winehouse and Roy Orbison have toured years after their deaths.

The trend is new but growing. One future scenario might be that CGI would let every career last forever. If so, our favorite performers never have to fade.

Roy Orbison's 2018 holographic tour included music performed by a full orchestra.

AI might be involved with writing in the future as well. Film director Oscar Sharp and researcher Ross Goodman worked with an AI program named Benjamin. They fed Benjamin scripts from popular drama and science-fiction films. The AI program learned what words and phrases showed up together. Benjamin used this knowledge to write a funny science-fiction movie. The film has been called weird and odd, but some people enjoy it.

Benjamin later tried to make an entire film in 48 hours. It wrote and directed the short film. It used scenes from earlier films. It changed the actors by digitally swapping their faces. It added voices and the soundtrack.

AI can't yet create a long story that makes sense. Someday it might. Then movies, TV shows, and books might be made by artificial intelligence. The technology should improve over time. It may be used more often in the future.

Film director Oscar Sharp used AI to create a movie in 2016.

USER TAKE OVER

On the other hand, maybe AI won't run the show. User-generated content (UGC) is big and growing bigger. UGC is made by regular people. It can include videos, photos, or other media. Anyone can create content and post it online.

With UGC, anyone can build a career on social media video platforms such as YouTube, Twitch, and others. On YouTube, people can share makeup tips, review movies or books, or simply chat. Twitch is mainly for video games. Players let people watch them play a game.

A few UGC stars make millions of dollars per year. Making money isn't easy, though. People need tens of millions of fans. Still, anyone can release a song or shoot a film. They don't need a big company behind them. Teens and young adults watch UGC more than older groups. The interest in UGC will likely keep growing. UGC could someday put big media companies out of business.

As of 2019, 7-year-old Ryan Kaji was one of the highest paid YouTube stars. In 2018 he earned $22 million dollars.

FACT
The top 3 percent of YouTube channels get 90 percent of the views.

TECHNOLOGY INSIDE US?

One way or another, we'll have plenty of entertainment content. We'll probably take our tech with us everywhere we go. We may even **embed** it into our bodies.

We already have embedded devices. Health devices can track problems and alert patients' doctors. Some experts think the future could see us using embedded tech for fun. Many teens surveyed said they would like a device embedded in their arm. The device could do everything that today's smartphones do, but it would be impossible to lose.

We must answer some questions before we become fully connected. How can you keep your data safe? You'll be tracked everywhere, at all times. Your parents, your school, or others will know where you are. They may be able to tell what you're doing. Would the convenience be worth the loss of privacy?

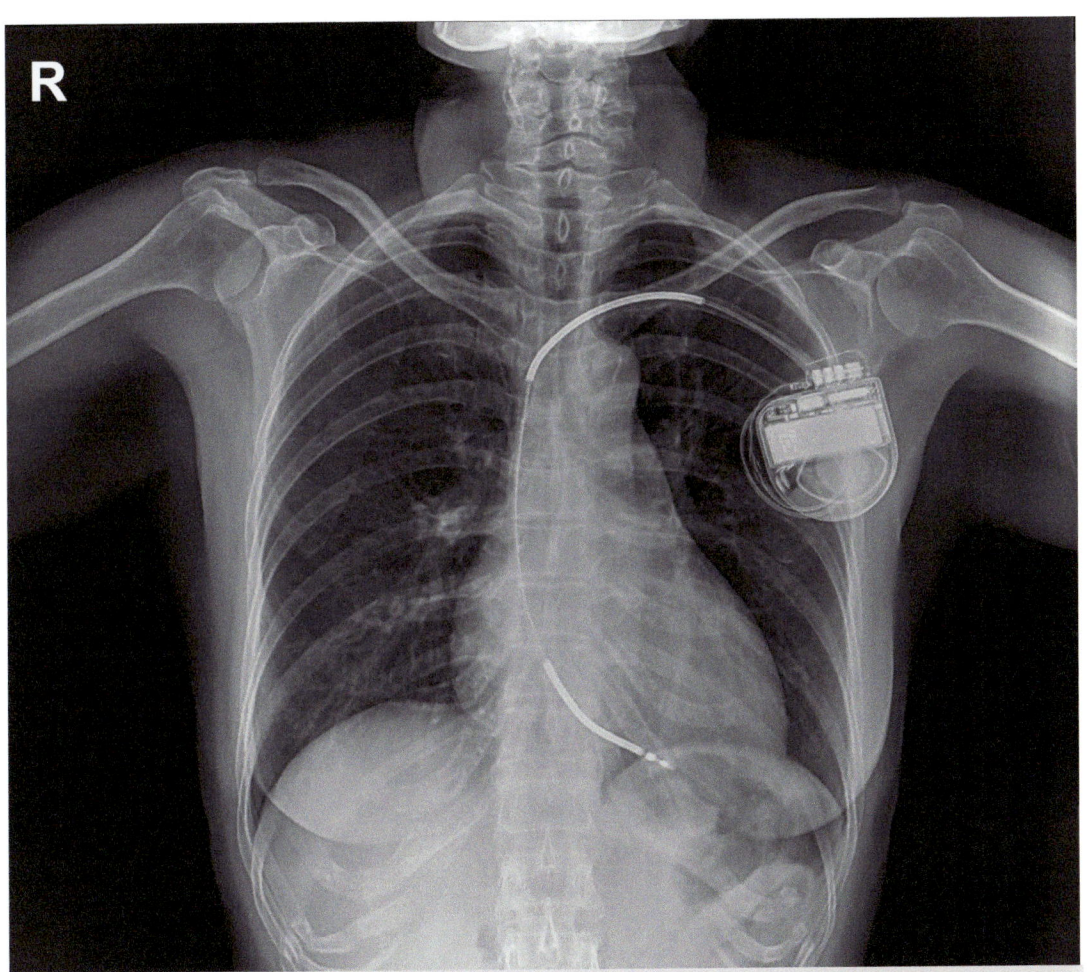

A pacemaker is an electronic device that can help control abnormal heart rhythms.

FACT

Body fluids are good at carrying electrical signals. Technology can use the body to send signals up to 30 feet (9 m).

CONNECTING OR DIVIDING?

From sharing stories around a campfire, to putting on plays and musical performances, to broadcasting on radio and TV, people have created more entertainment choices than ever before. In the future, technology will probably still be a big part of how we get our entertainment. We might wear glasses that show us augmented reality. We might have internet connections inside our bodies. We'll interact with AI. We could learn mainly through VR. We may even have robot friends.

People want to feel connected. They want real-life friends, online friends, and maybe robot friends. They want to hear and tell stories. That won't change, even if the technology does. Using entertainment to connect and unwind is part of what makes us human.

Live music is a form of entertainment that has withstood the test of time.

TIMELINE

1888 German scientist Heinrich Hertz demonstrates how to make radio waves.

1894 British scientist Oliver Lodge sends the first radio message.

1903 Thomas Edison produces the first silent movie with a real story line, *The Great Train Robbery*.

1925 The first crude TV images are shown at a London department store.

1927 The first movie with sound is released.

1928 The first known TV program is broadcast to four TV sets.

1932 The first TV station begins broadcasting.

1939 Televisions go on sale to the public.

1940 The first computer game is demonstrated at the World's Fair.

1940s Full-color films become common.

1948 Americans can watch TV shows from four networks.

1951 The first color program is broadcast, but only 12 TVs can show the color.

1952 Twenty million households in America have TV sets.

1954 Color TV sets with 15-inch screens sell for more than $1,000.

1976 3-D computer-generated imagery is first used in movies.

1993 Ninety-eight percent of American homes have at least one TV.

2004 Facebook starts and has 1 million users by the year's end.

2005 YouTube is founded.

2006 Twitter begins.

2010 Instagram and Pinterest begin. Facebook has more than 500 million users.

2011 Twitch begins, letting gamers stream themselves playing video games.

2015 The world has 15 billion internet-connected devices.

2017 Netflix introduces its first interactive TV show.

2020 The world has about 30 billion internet-connected devices.

GLOSSARY

augmented reality (AR) (AUG-men-tuhd ree-AL-uh-tee)—technology that overlays computer-generated data on a real-world environment

computer-generated imagery (CGI) (kuhm-PYOO-tuhr-JEN-uh-ray-tuhd IM-ij-ree)—digital graphics created by computers

data (DAY-tuh)—information or facts

embed (em-BED)—to place firmly in something

futures studies (FYOO-churz STUD-eez)—the study of possible and probable futures

Global Positioning System (GLOH-buhl puh-ZI-shuh-ning SISS-tuhm)—an electronic tool used to find the location of an object; often called GPS

hack (HAK)—to use a computer to gain access to data without permission

haptic feedback (HAP-tik FEED-bak)—the use of the sense of touch in electronic devices

hologram (HOL-uh-gram)—a three-dimensional image formed by light beams

machine learning (muh-SHEEN LER-ning)—the use of artificial intelligence to allow computers to learn

motion capture (MO-shuhn CAP-shur)—the process of recording the movements of people or objects

scenario (suh-NAIR-ee-oh)—an event that might happen

three-dimensional (THREE-duh-MEN-shun-uhl)—having length, width, and height; often shortened to 3-D

virtual reality (VR) (VUR-choo-uhl ree-AL-uh-tee)—a three-dimensional world created by a computer

READ MORE

Hennessey, Jonathan. *The Comic Book Story of Video Games: The Incredible History of the Electronic Gaming Revolution.* Berkeley, CA: Ten Speed Press, 2017.

Oxlade, Chris. *The History of Robots.* Chicago: Heinemann-Raintree, an imprint of Capstone Global Library, LLC, 2018.

Rotolo, Anthony J. *Gaming Technology: Blurring Real and Virtual World*s. San Diego: ReferencePoint Press, Inc., 2019.

INTERNET SITES

The American Widescreen Museum
www.widescreenmuseum.com/index.htm

Early Television Foundation and Museum
www.earlytelevision.org/

Mocomi Kids: The History of Movies
mocomi.com/history-of-movies/

Science Kids: Technology Facts
www.sciencekids.co.nz/sciencefacts/technology.html

INDEX

artificial intelligence (AI), 24, 28, 30, 32, 36, 38, 42
augmented reality (AR), 18, 19, 20, 42

computer-generated imagery (CGI), 34
computers, 4, 5, 6, 14, 18, 24, 26, 32, 34

futures studies, 6

games, 4, 5, 6, 10, 14, 18, 19, 20, 26, 28, 30, 38
Global Positioning System (GPS), 24

haptic feedback, 16, 22
holograms, 25, 34

internet, 6, 24, 31, 42

machine learning, 28
movies, 4, 6, 8, 12, 22, 24, 34, 36, 38
music, 4, 6, 24, 34, 38, 42

radios, 4, 42
robots, 30, 32, 42

smartphones, 14, 16, 18, 21, 40
social media, 12, 13, 38, 39

TV, 4, 6, 7, 8, 9, 10, 12, 22, 36, 42

user-generated content (UGC), 38, 39

virtual reality (VR), 14, 15, 16, 17, 18, 20, 22, 42